To all my children, those at home and those in my heart. I love you more than you'll ever know. We are forever connected. - J.C.

To B, A, and E – my favorite parts of every day. – C.M.

Published by Kids Grief Support
Text Copyright © 2022 by Jessica Correnti.
Illustrations Copyright © 2022 by Catie Maskell.
For information regarding permission contact the publisher at contact@kidsgriefsupport.com
A portion of the proceeds are donated to the Johns Hopkins Pediatric Palliative Care Department.
Library of Congress Cataloguing: 2022900802 Correnti, Jessica. Forever Connected / Maskell, Cate. p.   cm
Summary: Sibling grief, death/dying, parenting, pregnancy loss, Ages 3-8 years
ISBN: 979-8-9855882-0-0 (pbk)
ISBN: 979-8-9855882-1-7 (hc)
ISBN: 979-8-9855882-2-4 (e-book)
This book was typset in Caroni.
Illustrations were digitally painted in Adobe Photoshop.
Editor: Sirah Jarocki.
Book Design Consultant: MelindaMartin.me

FOREVER connected

Jessica Correnti, MS, CCLS

ILLUSTRATED BY Cate Maskell

Kids
Grief
Support

"Goodbye, brother. Have a good day!
Don't get into any trouble!" Luca said.

"Remember... your brother died. He no longer has
a heartbeat, breathes, or is physically here with us," his mother said.

"Yeah, but I still like to talk to him.
It makes me feel like he is still here," said Luca.

"I wear this necklace for the same reason.
It makes me feel close to him," she agreed.

"I like looking at his pictures.
For show-and-tell yesterday,
I brought the picture of me meeting
him at the hospital," said Luca.

"We have a lot of little ways to connect with him," his mother said.

"We also have
our candle
that we light on days
when we are
thinking of him.

"Even my coffee mug. It was
a gift given to me when we
said our first hellos and
last goodbyes at the hospital.

"We have many treasured items full of love and memories."

"Where is my real brother?" Ty questioned.

"This is your real brother. After we left the hospital, his body was put in a casket, which is a special wooden box that is placed in the ground under the grass," his father said.

"When can I see him again?" asked Ty.

"I'm sorry, Ty. I wish we could see him and hold him again,
but when someone dies, they never come back," explained his father.

"That makes me really sad."

"I know. Me too. We will always feel sad that he is not here with us. We will also always feel his love, no matter where we go. Let's go for a walk and look for things that make us think of him."

"I found a
heart-shaped rock, Dad.
That makes me think
of my brother."

"Look, a ladybug just landed on me.
It is said that ladybugs bring good luck,"
his father said.

"Look! Look! The sky! It's my sister saying hi!
Miss you! Love you! Wish you were here!
See you later!" Rowan cheered.

"Where is my sister?"
asked Mila.

"She died. When people die, their bodies are either buried
in the ground or cremated, which means the body is made into ashes.
When someone is dead, they do not feel any pain.
Her ashes are on the shelf. Even though she is not physically here,
we always feel her connection," their mom said.

"What kind of connection?"
asked Rowan.

"She can't touch us,"
Mila was sure.

"Sometimes little rainbows
glide across her pictures
on the wall as if she is
sending a warm hug.

"And the little piggy you both
carry around—your sister
snuggled her in the hospital.

"Those are little reminders that she was here
and continues to live on within us forever," said their mom.

"So it's like she is sending a little message?"
Rowan asked.

"Everyone has something special that makes them think of and feel close to their loved one who died.

"For some, it may be a place, song, word, number, or an object."

"Like the memory box
in my room!" said Rowan.

"Yes. For others it may be
the flitter of a butterfly,

a special flower,

an animal,

or simply looking at
a beautiful sky,"
their mom explained.

"Let's share what you have painted to show your connection to your sibling who died. Tell us about it," Ms. Aida requested.

"When my brother died,
my family kept finding acorns everywhere.
They gave me sparks of happiness even
when we were
feeling sad," said Ty.

"The day after my brother died,
there were tons of cardinals outside our window.
It felt like his way of saying, 'Hi, I'm here with you. I'm
okay!' I picked red to show how much I love him," said Luca.

"My sister's name means pearl. So, I painted pearls on a little piggy, like the one she had at the hospital," said Rowan.

"Rainbows make me think of my sister!" shared Mila.

"Such beautiful stories. Connected to your siblings, always," said Ms. Aida. "We miss them. We carry this great sadness and even greater love with us all at once. That love and connection live forever."

Note to Caregivers and Professionals

Acknowledgment

Caregivers: If you are purchasing this book for a bereaved child, I want to first let you know that I am so sorry that you are here. I am sorry that you have joined this 'child loss club' that no one ever wishes to join. It is unfair and gut-wrenching. You are not alone in this journey. Bereaved families stick together. I applaud you for being the amazing caregiver that you are by seeking out resources to help your bereaved child(ren) understand, process, and cope with the death.

Professionals: Thank you for your work with the forgotten grievers, bereaved siblings. Helping bereaved children cope with the reality of death is a privileged and sacred role.

How to Talk to Children about Death

Honest and Concrete Information: Children do best by being told the truth with simple, concrete language. It may seem harsh, but using the words *death, dying, and died* are recommended to prevent misconceptions from occurring. If a reason is known for the death, providing that in simple terms is also very helpful for understanding. When people choose to use euphemisms or softer language, children can often become confused or anxious.

Acknowledge Emotions: A big piece of supporting bereaved children is acknowledging feelings that come with this heavy experience. Help them identify and label the emotions they are feeling and feel free to show your own emotions. Showing your own emotions gives children the permission to do the same. Allow them to feel and express all emotions that come up unapologetically: joy, fear, sadness, anger, jealousy, guilt, etc. It is also very normal to experience many emotions at once, including contradicting emotions.

How to Help Children Process and Heal While Grieving

Follow their lead and play: Children process their world and experiences through play. Give them plenty of opportunities to play and process emotions. Do not be alarmed if they 'play through' and 'reenact' this death experience; this is normal and healthy.

Create connection with the child that died: Plant a garden together, make a candle, share pictures, create a memory book or video, talk to the child that died, and attend bereaved children support groups or memorial gatherings.

Seek out professional help: Contact Child Psychologists, Certified Child Life Specialists, Licensed Children's Grief Counselors, Licensed Play Therapists, and Licensed Clinical Social Workers for further support.

Jessica Correnti, MS, Certified Child Life Specialist

About the Author and Illustrator

Jessica Correnti has worked extensively with bereaved children within her professional role as a Certified Child Life Specialist at several children's hospitals. Her passion for supporting children going through difficult life experiences was amplified after she and her family personally went through several miscarriages and the stillbirth of their little girl, Maggie. She has a Bachelors in Education of Young Children with a minor in Psychology and a dual Masters in Healthcare Administration and Community Health. Jessica is the owner of Kids Grief Support, a private practice providing psychosocial support to grieving children and families. She hopes that every bereaved child is given the resources to process and heal while knowing they are heard, valued, and loved.

Connect with Jessica for further support and resources for your grieving child.

www.kidsgriefsupport.com

 @kidsgriefsupport

Cate Maskell is a commission-based artist from suburban Baltimore, MD. She loves creating art with pigments of all varieties but is especially drawn to the way watercolor behaves on paper. Cate fell in love with children's books, and the artwork within, at a young age. That love grew exponentially once she started a family of her own. To her, illustrations are an opportunity to strengthen the connection between the reader and the words on the page. Cate feels honored to use her illustrator role as a way to support parents, caregivers, and children cope with difficult life issues. Her goal is to create artwork that encourages quality time spent with each page, deepening the relationship between the message and the reader.

 cate@catebeforeamirror.com

 @catebeforeamirror

Photos by Julie Linz Photography

CPSIA information can be obtained
at www.ICGtesting.com
Printed in the USA
LVHW071243180922
728646LV00014B/876